SOUL MEDITATIONS

by Steve Thorp

Illustrated & designed by Ruth Thorp

SOUL MEDITATIONS

ISBN: 978-0-9928647-6-7

Published by Raw Mixture Publishing
The Granary, Middle Tancredston,
Haverfordwest, Pembrokeshire, SA62 5PX
www.rawmixture.co.uk

Typeset in Berylium

Printed by Gomer Press, Wales
on 100% recycled Cyclus Offset paper

A catalogue record for this book is
available from the British Library.

Raw Mixture Publishing

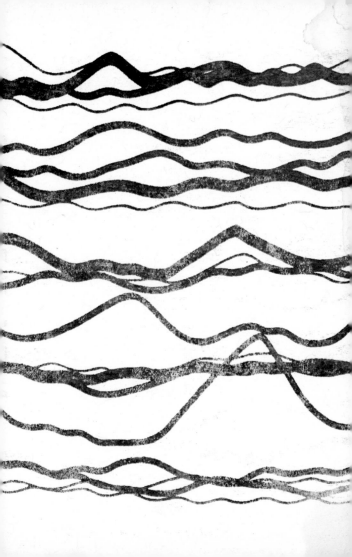

To practice a soul meditation is
to be open to presence; to follow
what the soul whispers:

Step one: **notice**
Step two: **breathe**
Step three: **accept**
Step four: **sustain**
Step five: **internalise**
Step six: **utilise**
Step seven: **connect**
Step eight: **activate**

To activate is to create your self in
the world's image. The final step,
then, is to **imagine**.

PRELUDE

Forget sitting on a cushion – *this* is meditation:

Stand in the cool breeze on an early summer's day.

Allow the three-dimensional, multi-sensory world to meet you. See moving slabs of shadow cool and darken. Hear birdsong and insect-chatter so keenly that you know *for sure* what they are saying.

Walk with the rhythm of your heartbeat until the earth, too, drums along to your march through the world. Touch the sand and the sea and the sky all at once. Be truly at the edge of things.

Look into the eyes of another person (a baby, a stranger), another creature (a beady-eyed jackdaw). Imagine the sense they have of you. Use your skin and your body to guide you. Become aware of how you know you are approaching emptiness or immensity – just by the blind sense of it.

Examine the earth with love; watch it move with you throughout the day. Watch it wake and wane; feel your body mirror its rhythms. Hear the smallest whisper in the tiniest wilderness. Learn that awe is in a giant sky, and in a seed pod fallen to the ground.

Breathe all of this in each day. *This* is meditation.

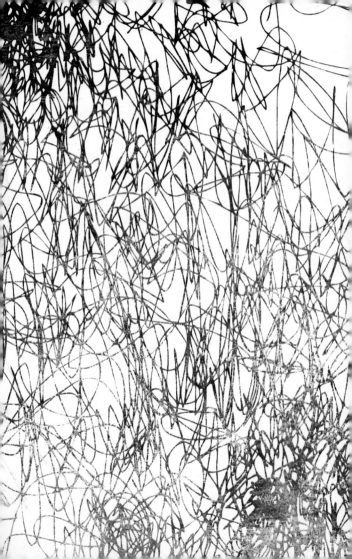

...of course, sitting on a cushion can be a good place to learn perseverance and the ability to stay with discomfort.

However, the everyday, here-and-now needs paying attention to.

We can do this walking, standing, sitting, bending. In silence or in a hubbub. In a quiet room, busy workspace or city street. On a march for progress, a windy coast-path or sitting at our desk.

Or when standing for something...

meditation #1

× constellation × *It is a cool quiet morning. The sky is silver. The birds are fighting over scraps on the road outside. There is the deep throb of a plane flying over. I immerse myself in these senses for a moment.*

I feel the warmth of the newly lit fire at my back. My body is aching from the hard surf I fought a day ago. I feel the weak and strong points in my body. I am aware of my ageing. Moment by moment, I sense myself change.

My mind is settling after the colourful assault on the senses that is waking. My dreams fade. I am aware of a flutter of emotion – a little anxiety. I feel strength and determination. I sit with these for a moment.

All these levels coexist. I am a constellation. I am aware of my awareness shifting from one to another. If I am careful, I can start to do this with gentle willpower. Sometimes I spin off somewhere. I bring myself back.

I have a conversation. Feel the relational waves pull lightly between us. I reach out, then come back to the awareness that has been building.

Beneath all this: a sense of preparation, and a hint of joy.

meditation #2

× layers of light ×

My back is aching. My eyes are hurting, My feet are chilled. I need to stretch. I will wait till I have completed this work.

I close my eyes and let this creative hour soak into me. I notice it seep like a smile and glance to look at what I have created. I am satisfied.

I adjust to become more comfortable and sit with it. The day has been dark and rainy one hour, sunny the next. At this moment, the sun is glancing in through the window, washing the walls with light, illuminating the corners of the room.

At last, I breathe into all this.

I sit for a few moments, touching all these subtle layers. Each fine stratum of air carries clouds of fragments. Each is a mote in the sun's stream. There are millions of others that do not come to light.

The wind feeds the fires, blows the clouds, gives an aural backdrop to my day. The breezy light changes everything.

× timescales ×

I sit alone for an afternoon. A timescale of seconds or millions of years. The first disappears before it is noticed. The second is only ever a conceptual reality.

Chase the first. Imagine the second.

The first timescale is like surfing. Sitting here, I can generate the excitement of sliding down a wave – second upon gnarly second. At any time, I could be interrupted and be turned over by circumstance. Wipe-out.

The second timescale is like falling endlessly. After a while I stop flailing and slow down so each moment can be noticed.

The first falls into the second.

Time circles itself like groundswell travelling the oceans.

meditation #4

× past times × *This morning I decide to waymark a moment in my life. My intention is to interrupt the habitual in order to accept the inevitable. To create a memory that allows both past and future to be part of the present.*

And of my 'self'.

The past plays like a film. Edited. In scenes. I notice that, for the most part, these memories no longer have emotions attached, do not evoke a response, except, sometimes, a wistful smile or frown.

Some of these scenes evoke a kind of filmic nostalgia: a complex that a fleeting dream image or sensory experience can elicit.

This way, the past exists in me this morning. I shuffle in the duvet, and stretch into the day.

× two futures ×

Project. This is the film of the future.

There are two futures, both of them mine.

One, I create. In it, I am free, have limitless possibility.
The second is predestined. It is where I am heading.

Both are true.

This meditation is carefully crafted by imagination.
I must listen so carefully to the distant future that I
hear its faint whisper. It heads back towards me like
an arrow, speeding into my past. Habits are destroyed;
avoidances and fears taken out with surgical precision.

I lift my head and face the storm, step into a cascade
of freezing water, speak my mind to the most daunting
adversary.

It is what I am destined for. It is what I have created.

meditation #6

× home hub ×

The rhythm of a travelled life – mindfully lived – carries the joy of homecoming. A familiar hum in the best of places. Layers of everyday sound. An implicit sense of fit and belonging.

Sounds: Tapping keyboard. Faint fire-crackle. Dishwasher rattle. The tap and crunch of breakfast. Voices. Spring sounds seeping in from outside – strimming and mowing, digging and doing, reconstruction and rebirth.

Sights: Stone walls. Freshly painted wooden stairs. Clothes drying in front of the stove. Homely furnishings that mould to my body. Rugs, boxes and lamps. All familiar. Outside, a small flock of sheep wander the village and jackdaws watch over it.

Feelings: Tiredness – heavy – edged contentedly with left-over dreaming. Love for place and people. A loosening and easing. Welcome acceptance and gentle engagement. Joy.

I breathe quietly into this belonging. Here is the foundation for a necessary energy of activism and calling. Replenish and rejuvenate. Each week, from here, I grow out to touch the world again.

× soft body ×

Sometimes the body carries the resistant habits of the mind. This morning my body, soaked with the tiredness of travelling, wants to sleep. The mind's jabber of 'should' seeps into my limbs making them restless and taut.

First, as always, I breathe into the animal in me. Give each part of me permission to rest. First my fingers and toes succumb and then my legs and arms. Then just as the tension had seeped into my torso, it starts to leach out.

It is always the rhythm that is transformed as it unfolds into leaden softness.

Soon my active mind (murmuring 'shoulds' and lists of things to make and do) is surrounded.

Then even that surrenders, and the words of this meditation drift away.

The 'soft animal'* in me dozes for a season.

* "You only have to let the soft animal of your body
  love what it loves"

Wild Geese, Mary Oliver

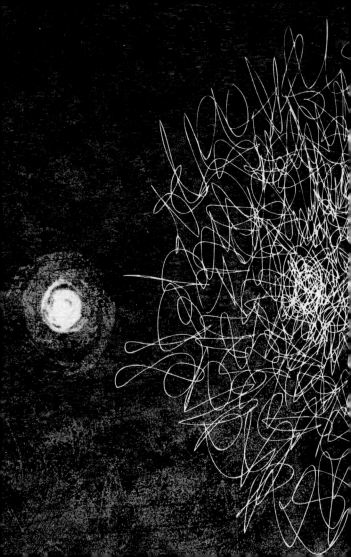

Of course, 'I' will always be
there somewhere. It would take
a particular type of unworldly
compulsion to claim that this can
ever really be transcended.

Meanwhile there is a world to be
met.

Your task is to meet the world in
the self, and the self in the world.

And the world in other selves.

And the soul in all of this...

× meditation jewel ×

Imagine. Visualise. Sense.

Close eyes. Walk down a pathway out of a dream. Enter a forest. Walk among tumbled trunks and rising boles.

Look down. A billion tiny lifeforms scuttle and feed here. This is your world. It is more alive than you have ever imagined. Sense this life.

Lift your head and look up. The canopy filters a warm sun and dapples the ground. Let the sounds of the forest come to awareness. Distinguish the birdsong and the voices of the breeze.

Walk on. Each tree, branch, twig and leaf is a moment of awareness and experience. Recall it now – whether it sits in the past or in the future.

Sit for a while in the forest. Then walk out into a grassy clearing. The sunlight is bright and warm, but even in the brightness there is a light in the centre that shines out. Walk towards it. Slowly. Taking time to sense its energy and power. Look down. There is a jewel.

Hold it in the palm of your hand. Cradle it and let its light colour you. Stay a while. Know you can always return. This is your forest. Your world. Your universe. A constellation of you.

meditation #9

× between two × *Sit together and talk a while. A moment will arrive that one of you can mark with a quiet word. Then breathe, together, deep into what emerges between you. You will be the guide.*

Emotion flickers on the face of the other. A tear might fall. You can tell they are somewhere else: inside, beyond, in their past or future. They may be in that moment now. Notice everything. Encourage them, gently, to notice everything, to keep breathing into whatever emerges.

Notice the way their body settles into itself. It is different now from the animated human who conversed with you. Now the body becomes animal. Moment by moment, it is sustained by breath and imagination. Something subtle emerges between you. Settle into the attenuated rhythm of this 'being with' (which might, for a moment, be called love, and may look as if it is, for them, a surrender).

Allow the cycle to complete. You will know this when your companion shifts and meets your gaze with a settled finality. Now you can breathe into the depth of your giving, for you have also been to an extraordinary place. You will have the blithe knowing of the altruist.

Then it is their turn to take your place.

meditation #10

× to be tempted ×

Amidst the crowded marketplace of spiritual gurus, and the ways personal growth is wrapped in increasingly esoteric and academic concepts, it is as well to remember the true simplicity of spirit.

If spirit is to have a place in our future, it will come through the still small voice we hear when all else has fallen away.

So do not ask, 'what does it mean to be human?'
And do not ask, 'who or what is God?'
Ask, instead, 'what does it feel like to be here, in this small moment?'

Be tempted to be yourself, in other words. Be tempted to know yourself. Be tempted to make peace with yourself.

Light a small flame and – your face illuminated in candle-light – look out into your world.

Listen out for other small voices and speak with them. Reach out through the cloak of this comforting silence into the community of souls.

× to be grounded ×

Sometimes I feel weary with the world.

This is an appropriate response to this crazy place. We make it crazy, we humans, with our frantic certainty and need to make a mark.

Sometimes I also get weary with words. There are so many of them – tweeted, blogged, spoken, shouted, written, sung – words, more often than not, wasted.

And there are too many ideas, and not enough big ones. This means that we humans have our heads in the clouds (or stuck some other place) for much of the time.

So today I want to champion a grounded silence. One that does not feel it necessary to dispute this or challenge that. One that does not need to have a lightbulb moment or make a million or save the world.

Today I just want to be in the world.

meditation #12

× **walking** × *Put one foot in front of the other. That's all you have to do to start any journey.*

Get a rhythm going: This foot, then that; this side, then that; this breath then that. Like drumbeat and bass under a quiet melody, let this roll for a while. Notice how the day's clamour starts to fall away a little. Don't force this, just watch it as it happens.

When you're in a groove, start to notice what's around. For me, last evening, it was scattered wood in the bridleway; sheep in the field behind the bank, staring at a trudging stranger. Then onto the moor and the rutted, winter ground.

Breathe in. Check rhythm. Stride on.

Birds are everywhere. A peewit calls. Thirty crows swirl through the sky – though the starling clouds have long disappeared. Down by the stream – flash, flash – a pair of woodpeckers dart across the eyeline. Then you turn back west to see the evening trees silhouetted against a giant sun-washed sky.

Follow what you see. Let the sounds of the journey enter the rhythm. This foot then that; this side then that; this breath then that.

meditation #13

× running × *Up and out, into the afternoon.*
Slap foot one, slap foot two. Build the rhythm, feel the breath:
the body rocking from side to side. Slap foot, slap foot. Up, up
and out into the hills.

The road disappears under your feet. Running shoes
enfold feet like slippers. The cold air goes deeper as you
climb. The rasping in your lungs has its own rhythm
now – joining feet, heart and pumping arms as you climb.

Pause. Drink in the air and the land spread before you.
Feel the cold sun on your skin.

Up, up and out, into the afternoon – then down the
hills. Sprint and stretch. Extend and reach. Heels land,
toes land. Breath thickens. Heart coheres, thoughts align.
Senses deepen, breath thickens.

Slap foot, slap foot. Left then right. This side then that.
This breath then that. Sprint and stretch. Uphill now, to
the end of the run.

Up, down and back into the afternoon.

At the heart of a meditation is the breath. And the earth is always carried on the wind.

Wind blows the soul to place. Place is where we are rooted. We root ourselves by breathing and noticing.

When we notice, we can breathe and gain courage. Courage means we can do this thing.

En-couragement is to make the heart strong.

meditation #14

× gentle breath ×

Wake each morning: things are never the same.

Sometimes the stark brightness of the damage we have
wrought on each other and on our world is at the
forefront. The first response is despair. Can you weave
this into anger and resistance – and the emergence of
poetic alternatives?

At other times, the morning is warm and bright – full
of buzz, hum and rustle. Each grass-blade moves in this
shuffle of life. Every watching animal-eye is aware. The
first response is wonder. If you are observant enough,
you may also catch the faint current of connectedness
between our own life and these others.

Then there are mornings when you wake from
broken sleep. Nights of visitation. Dreams, obsessions,
transcendence. The first reaction might be panic, but
you can still enter the day with engagement and activity.
Frenzy turns to imagination; is transformed into the
small ways we might change our world.

Passionate mornings in which you love – fiery colours.
And quiet pastel mornings you wake into with gentle
breath – and thank the world for being within you.

× returning ×

I have been away.

I need to feel the sand between my toes again; the edge of the ocean chill my heels. I need to be free of shoes, waistbands and the constrictions of time. Just for a while. Just for enough time to loosen up the present moment so it is there again – that small shining echo just within my reach (reach, reach...).

Here is now. The moment. And now. It tingles and warms and it gives me space and imagination. "The real meditation is how you live your life," wrote John Kabat-Zinn.

I try to live mine quietly. And with wild surges and the joyful whoosh of the remembered child.

Words connect to moment, sand and salt ocean; to the tingling air, the warmth of the meditation; to the hopeful vision of a coming transition.

Moment connects to the colours of the wind and the naming of the summer hillside. Sand connects to a million voices – all life-sparks begun in a day – so the song of my return will be sung wildly for me.

meditation #16

× time × *Warily I step into a dream. It will not spare me. In this world there is no ego to temper the story. The only saviour is waking – though then the world is lost forever. A no-win situation.*

Time is lost. Time is told. Time is the unfolding of old stories. Time is the frozen moment into which we all eventually fall. Time is the missing dimension of dream and recall.

Memory is woven through the dream. The tapestry of time woven from a golden thread. An age ago I played in sunshine; I danced in snow; I flew down sandy hills as tall as mountains.

Time trips us up; tips us towards the falling. Time is the one thing we hold onto, as if it were clay, as if we could craft it into a new life, to dream the moulding of time.

To stave off memory and the crumbling tricks it plays.

× a spell × *Somewhere, in the midst of loneliness, magic can be found.*

People sit in their own worlds.

They are delineated by their souls, and by the teeming boundary of their skin.

First, experience the deep interior and a separation from billions of other material selves.

Can you then carve your hands through the physicality of the air and guide the wind to soothe this pain of isolation? In your eyes is a longing you have buried deep. Each tear you shed is a reminder of the flood to come; of the distance you have to swim down to gather pearls.

This spell brings us together. Words to make friends; subtle gestures to make peace. Drawn lines of exactitude and endowment. The honing of self – through biochemical alchemy – into love.

Could you ever love this mage – this scientist of the soul? Or is the shaman always destined to live at the edge of things?

meditation #18

× falling × *I have fallen into a grey evening. The rain is washing away colours. All that remains is one sorry foxglove, leaning heavily; its few remaining purple bells dripping.*

My vision has faded. My body has tired. My muse has vanished.

Outside, in the garden, the froth of grasses on the top of the wall sways sorrily in a damp summer breeze. The light rain has fallen forever, as the river rises towards drowning.

It is a melancholy time. A shrinking moment.
An in-folding.

The shrinking of the day has begun. Perhaps this is what life will be like now? Perhaps the omen of this grey-washed face is all that is promised?

This falling away of expectation will be stark relief. This will be the end – though it may mean a happiness of sorts.

× the noise behind ×

The noise behind the world is what keeps us from our natural selves. Even here, where it seems so peaceful, the layer beneath is full of buzz and bleep, hum and grumble.

Sometimes sitting in what we take for silence only reveals this peculiar, modern, human stratum – an archaeology of the aural soul. How far to dig down to reach the sounds our ancestors heard? Voices we catch a hint of when we are away from traffic, fridge and internet?

We are left with the shuffle and rustle of small creatures and the calls of larger ones. And the silence we thought was silence is filled with life, sound and warning.

Scraping away layers, we meet a deeper quiet. Perhaps the task now shifts from archaeology to palaeontology – sifting carefully through the strata of the wilderness, to see and hear what emerges next?

So, stand still in the remotest place you can find and imagine you are listening to the beginning. There is nothing to hear except what was always here.

The world. The wild. Indifferent existence.

× quiet and fuzzy ×

Quiet and fuzzy.

That's what I've been like for the past two weeks.

Quiet can be good, but I can be taken too deeply inside a version of me that is locked into a small room of worry, thinking and loss. Fuzzy is a state like static: white noise of body and mind that acts as a barrier to clarity.

Tinnitus of the soul.

How to move beyond this?

Wait. Notice. Trust your intuition that there is a clearer, more engaged place in the fleeting sunlight of emerging summer. Trust that loss is only a phenomenon of history; that the counterpoint is a promise of love and connection.

Quiet and fuzzy is enveloping – grey-white and muffled. Sometimes, clear blue and fierce orange lie beyond the cloud. And a free and joyful shout to celebrate the day.

× a paradox of emptiness ×

Inside we yearn to give ourselves to emptiness. What holds us back is attachment and necessity. Paradoxically, emptiness carries both fear and potential – what it might mean to give up everything.

Even writing this gives me a tightness. I move towards the security of the tangible. I have relationships and feel love. I have new beginnings and treasured histories. The familiar is now a comforting enhancement.

Can these familiar things hold emptiness? Can the paradox complete itself?

Perhaps I can be empty, even as I fill myself with loving attention? Perhaps I can be empty, as a poem emerges, unbidden, from within? Perhaps I can be empty, as I stand in the garden and look towards the hills?

As *this* moment empties out, what flows back in is tentative and intriguing. It is small, mysterious and utterly undimmed.

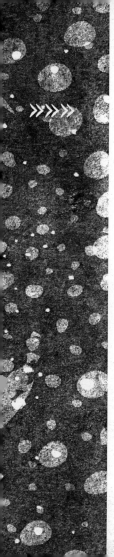

Shadows are one half of the self.

Meditation must acknowledge them, and sometimes go deep within these submerged and murky regions.

So, when you reach a place where the pain hits, or the world seems to be screaming, you will need courage to meditate your way in.

To stay with it. To come out the other side. Where there might be something like joy waiting.

Which is about as good as it gets...

× **night breath** × *Night breath is ghost in the room; the shifting shape of dreamtime.*

Storytime for the soul. Meditation for a different world. Metaphors for dying are placed just out of memory's reach, so you have to work hard to live by their injunctions.

A stream bubbles through. Gilled, you breathe from aerated channels in the mind. You swim dangerously close to waking.

For a moment you are aware of the room; its chilling air invites you. So you snuggle back into the layers and name each distinct image that flashes through the night. The ghosts are back and you greet them.

A tree is endlessly high; invites you to fly to its distant canopy – a speck set in blue clarity. You choose to climb instead. You will not go far tonight. You feel defeated. You feel elated.

You wake, too soon, into the ghost of the waking morning.

× this morning, the rain ×

This morning, the rain came. It has been a constant companion this summer, like a friend who stays too long and behaves inappropriately. Now everyone just smiles wryly.

It is too late now to have a summer of any significance. We accept that October is coming, with its familiar storms, the sound of rain hammering on the skylight and wind moaning through the trees.

Only the heavy heat feels a little like summer.

And then there is the settling. Of grief, and of drowning in summer storms. A sense of being split between seasons. Of lightness and joy versus heavy drip-dropping from the tree canopy.

As one generation looks back and yearns for a second childhood, another smiles and chuckles at the promise of light summer.

This morning the rain is love and loss. The world, once heavy grey, is bright again. Shafts of light bounce from white walls. The wind plays with the overgrown grasses like crowds of unruly children.

For now, they forget winter's dying and their smiles light up the world.

meditation #24

× yesterday's sky ×

When we wake the sky is silver. It could have been a grey morning but the air feels fresh. It is early, and the blue of the day will not wash through the sky for an hour.

Then the breakfast sky is blue, warmed nicely like croissants and coffee eaten outside in the light, late summer breeze. Flaked crumbs fall like September leaves.

At the beach, the tide comes in, drawing a thin cloud with it, like long smoke. As we walk, crows fight with a peregrine – stooping, falling – watched from above by a steady buzzard.

The sky clears. The sea turns from grey to blue and we fall into the water like laughing children.

Blue dies towards evening. The sky stays clear and, at midnight, we sit out looking up towards clouds of stars and constellations; staring from this earth, deep into the history of the universe.

× quiet light ×

Sometimes quiet has a texture. It feels so physical that all other sounds are just layered on top, like paint on canvas.

Silence feels heavy, grounded and necessary. Over it I hear the clacking of this keyboard, the wind, the hum of electronic devices, the creaking of the house and the thin whine of the mosquito that has been bothering me the past two days!

The texture of this quiet day is like deep water. I lower myself into it and feel lifted, buoyant even. As I type, the wind drops and sunlight comes through the windows – a paler light than last week, somehow – finding its own place in the layers of sound.

It is as if the sun changes the weight of quietness. As if there is an equation to be derived from this fleeting relationship that science has so far missed.

Yet how can you write an equation for the soul?

meditation #26

× **journey** × *Over the sea are grey columns*
and veils of cloud. Beyond them shines an orange light. If I
could walk through, I would be carried high into the jewel
of a sky.

Yet I am stuck. The rubber tyres hug the tarmac, and I
track the dying of the day from this road that splits the
land.

At the sight of the ragged peaks at Wolfscastle, I turn
towards the hills, and here the clouds gather ominously
for their spectacular, nocturnal jamboree. Tonight, up
there, there will be a rumpus and a brouhaha.

The winds will blaze fiercely across the uplands.

Creatures like and unlike me – livestock, beasties,
strange phantoms and vague ideas of carnal form – will
cower in the sheltered spots and crannies, all of us
seeking shelter among old stones.

The ancient bluestones, shining with the dying light of
the fractured sky, hold slow promise.

It will take a storm of epic proportions to break their
resolve.

 One thing we all learn from
meditation is that there is more to
the world than we can ever see.

Everything is born of flesh, bone,
imagination, archetype.

Even the land is imagined as
creaturely. Each lifeform
re-imagined as a soul in itself.

(Fly. Spider. Sparrow. Peregrine.
Kite. Fox. Wolf. River Dolphin.)

And the earth? The earth holds
all our stories.

meditation #27

× water world ×

I live in water. Smooth and sleek I slide between fronds of weed. There are millions of tiny bubbles and I climb into one and rise up until it pops.

I fall again and breathe in the water's cool buoyant story. Water rising. Waves breaking. Oceans carrying the life we were born from.

I sing of swimming.

Fish share my world. This one stares into my mind to see the very start of time. This one swims alongside as I travel the stream of words that tumble through my head as I learn to breathe.

If I can breathe in water, then anything is possible.

My slow body sinks, heavy into the silt, as the grey sands shift, absorb me.

My water is my disappearance. My transformation is complete.

× sit down and fly ×

Sit down as I tell you this. You will need to be sitting.

The world is not as it seems. It exists only between the cracks of your imagination. It is created at night by the godhead of dreams. This intricate lacing of reality and intelligence only lasts as long as your attention does, then – poof! – it disappears.

Did you not know this? Did you think that the ground you stand upon is a solid entity? It is a mistake many of us make, as we measure, mould and craft our lives from the solid stuff.

Stardust is anything but solid. It is not even a quantum event. It is the ethereal whisper of eternity, and an infinite cloud of possibility.

Sit down as I tell you this. Now, you will need to learn to fly.

× dark matter ×

I let out a breath that I have been holding for days.

The sun is still absent. I look out on a familiar scene:
The road as it loops down towards the moor. The tree
that stands on the patch of green. A damp grey wall of
a sky.

There is a flat world out there. It is possible to fall off
the edge. I know. I am on that edge right now and
staring down to a dark river, a deep valley and a dark,
deep promise of falling.

Dark matter flows through my veins, inverts me. Today
is a day of holding and breathing out. This eases my
yearning to change things.

It makes no difference to the world – no more than
praying does. No more than dancing, talking or
hunting. No more than dreaming does.

There is a flat world out there. I breathe in courage, turn
at the edge and begin the long walk to the other side.

× winter butterfly ×

Around me, a cloud of winter butterflies is rising. Ice crackles in their wings, as the wind blows them from the hills to the sea.

It is a dreaming, an inversion. A stream of static consciousness unfolding like murmurations of white starlings settling on the trees outside the door.

In the world, a relentless wind pours around this house. It is well crafted, warm, comfortable. Outside, the wind and the rain soak into brick and stone. Inside this quiet white envelope, silence is held.

There is an echo in this home, that takes time to seep into the walls' memory. Her laughter is still tinkling; her indignant baby shouts reverberate. This house – born again this winter – always remembers her when she returns.

I have always loved that word: chrysalis. It has the comfort of resting and the promise of growing.

The winter butterfly has left today, but she will come back soon.

× sun and stone ×

Sun and stone reawaken. Sit and notice.

The year takes a pause, then blows again onto the shore. Sand and silver sea – the glister of tides.

A fishing boat nestles close into the harbour wall, waiting for the new opportunity. Water slaps against the hull. Seals shelter in their port in a storm.

Hewn rock tumbles. Winter responds to your question with a stone promise. Salt cakes your face. You hide from the early light, and watch the year flicker into life – wake and grow.

The sun dazzles; it falls like breathing each day into the ocean. Rises like breathing each morning over the stones.

Your breath is like the sun. Your life is a shining stone picked from the beach. And this one. And this one.

Sit and notice as your year awakens.

meditation #32

× endless storm ×

This is the storm. This is love. This is the end that everyone comes to. This is the flight that everyone makes. We all come back home, eventually.

Where is home? Where does the storm return to?

You are the wind within you. Does this answer satisfy the curiosity of disruption?

When there is a lull, we imagine the worst is over. The truth is that the worst is to come – but it will not finish us off just yet.

Each of us has an ending worthy of a scratched mark on the stone, a simple acknowledgement of the passing of time. A small celebration. None of us deserve anything less.

One day, our gentle spirit will diminish and the breeze will die. There will be a stillness before the wind begins its furious work again.

This is the endless storm. Everyone dies. Everyone lives. There is joy in the passing. There is a smiling silence and a flood of love.

What can be done?

With clarity, courage,
breath and presence you
can do what you are
supposed to do.

That original push and pull;
the tug and toil of soul.

Ask what needs to be done.
See what needs to be done.
Be encouraged. Hold courage.

If you can do these things,
there will always be hope
glimmering in the
shadows.

× wings are optional ×

We are all flying now – but wings are optional. Air rises on a breathtaking furnace of vanity and carries us with it. Effortlessly entitled, we see no need to be grounded as we soar between worlds.

In this space, nothing is as it seems. The eternal becomes a blip in time. The infinitesimal becomes the infinite. There is a pulse in which everything – and nothing – is held.

We should understand that we are rushing things. The white light of our evolution has blinded us. The way of the universe is slower, more solid, than we ever imagined. We disappear into its fullness.

The fallacy is that the whorl ascends into illuminance.

We will not be flying for long if the earth, in her rage at our destruction, brings us back down. Then we will watch on helplessly as the other animals run free.

There is a way. It requires us to give up the dream of flying.

× starting over ×

Places that matter never look the same.

Perhaps this is because, when we are in them, we have our eyes wide open. Or perhaps it is the combining of 'me' with this place that is important – the belonging, in other words.

Walking on this beach is always different. Every day the sky changes, the beach shifts.

Today, the beach is covered with stones, dragged down from the breakwater by the high tide. The sky, uniform grey for the past four days, breaks into colour. The sea carries dancing lights from the setting sun.

This place matters and matters most because of the people I walk with – those with whom I celebrate this shining beginning.

So I am hopeful – even at this ragged time. At this late hour, we may still soften our stance, notice the changing landscape – and choose to belong.

× choose earth ×   *Up to light and*
transcendence or down to the good dark earth?

If you choose transcendence, promise the earth that
your feet won't leave its fertile ground for long. If
you choose earth, never give up hope of becoming
something for all of us.

If you cannot make the first promise, choose earth –
there is more at stake than your personal salvation.

If you choose earth, you are siding with the material,
corporeal, sensory, evidential – the animal. Putting
spirit, belief and the possibility of illumination and
rapture aside, means being an ally with the good in
other people, your fellow lifeforms and the land that
sustains them.

So choose. Find a balance if you think you are capable
of sustaining it, but choose a downward path if you
doubt you have the resolve to return to earth when you
have been flying among bright clouds.

And in the loamy depths, your soul might surprise you
– sparking into new light and bright flame.

meditation #36

× interface × *I like that there are only a few inches of stone and wood between me and the world. I like that I can walk out of my door and share the lanes with sheep and foxes, jackdaws and peregrines.*

I like that the sky is silver in the evenings and the sun sets over the hills in an entirely different way each day. I like the soft air and the speckled black-night sky and the warmth of the fire against my back as I write.

I like the writing of this and the ease with which my fingers move over the keyboard. I like that my words can be yours as soon as I press 'post'. I like that I can speak to a friend through this light and easy silver machine, and ask her how she is doing – though we haven't met for months.

I like surfing. Both kinds. Cold sea stinging warm skin. The smooth euphoria of a long glassy ride. Waves of information available as I paddle out into the world. Riding the new.

I like being still in the midst of real and virtual worlds.

I catch my breath.

I like knowing that it might just be a very good time to be alive.

× airflow × *On the headland, stiff breeze blows away my waiting and the world is alive again. A stiff walk up and down the steep paths and gullies and my body is in touch with its animal. The turquoise sea is frilled with white and the gulls and crows soar and spiral.*

On the path, I nearly step on a small grass snake, barely moving in the sun. Further on, scattered feathers mark the spot where a bird has been prey. Around another turn, the seasonal wildflowers twinkle in the sunlight. Bluebells, sea thrift, campion and quill.

Above, against the sun, I see a dark mark flying. At first, I think it is a raven, but it feels as ominous as a storm cloud. The crows crowd around, stabbing, then the bird arcs down. The wind stills and the air hums at the speed of it.

It is a peregrine, nesting in the nearby cliffs. It sends all the other birds into a spin at the twitch of a wing.

It soars effortlessly, then stoops through the squalling wind. The dark smudge in the sky becomes a tawny-brown speck of fearsome beauty travelling alone in its own airflow.

meditation #38

× warriors of love ×

Sometimes we feel as if exhaustion can take us – this time, finishing us off – chewing us up and spitting us out as empty husks with no more energy for any kind of activism.

When this happens, our art becomes safe and stagnant – words and artefacts no longer having value. Just souvenirs for those who pass by to purchase.

Sustaining soulful, artful, joyful, imaginative, social and ecological engagement is essential for our wellbeing – but also carries enchantment and a promise to the world.

And each time a band of dreamers meets to sing, dance and share conversation, the exhaustion of impossibility falls away. Each time we touch deep into our souls to articulate some universal vision, something stirs.

Each time we dare to imagine there is a better way – even amidst the mess we have made of the world – we find our power, practice and deep knowledge rising.

Meditate on this: It may be impossible to stay exhausted when you choose to be a 'warrior of love'*.

---

* "the exhausted should therefore clear/the stage for new dreamers – for warriors of love, justice/ and enlightenment."
Mental Fight by Ben Okri.

What truth is not:
belief; individual experience;
meaningless generalisation;
assertion without evidence;
evidence without context; old
stories told literally; new stories
told only in hope...

What truth might be:
felt as much as thought; hinted at
in the universal; found in the space
between wonder and curiosity;
a sense of knowing drawn
widely; old and new stories told
imaginatively...

What truth is: beautiful.

× the mind poet ×

The mind makes poetry like the earth makes mountains. This tells us more about uncertainty than about knowledge.

Between the polarities of knowledge and faith, determinism and free-will, lies the instinct of poetry. Not all of us will be poets in the literary sense, but we can *all* bring a poem from inside that tells a story of our daily lives.

Stare at the sky and imagine the world that the falcon inhabits. See, you are already a poet!

The birds live in a different world. The avian eye sees things that we do not; yet the bird brain is not (as far as we know) a poetic one.

When poetic images fly, they gather in great murmurations of chaotic whispers. They surprise and delight us; sometimes make us shiver with unwanted recognition.

This tells us something about the futility of certainty.

× modern life ×

Early this morning, I came tumbling out of sleep into the waking dusk. It is too early, there is too much still shaking around inside. I need the grounding of meditation to calm me.

When modern life goes wrong, our psychological resilience is tested. Even when we are doing well. Even when we have kept going through the smog, fog, noise and clatter, there are layers between us and the real.

Like silt layers after a flood, they dry and harden and we can mistake the dull and moulded shape of these things for the sharp, clear stuff of life.

So, through the veil of existence and the plastic noise of a life, can we keep glimpsing the earth? From a train or a car window, from looking around while walking – *quick quick quick* – to our next assignation.

Can we be *with* the air and earth – even as we are waiting for something else to happen?

meditation #41

× **wild night** × *On a wild night, even when wrapped in the civilising comfort of crisp sheets there is something more terrifying than dreams: a dark and boisterous nether life emerging just after the silent time.*

Even in the frantic city there is that wild time, when foxes walk along bitumen channels under street lights that illuminate nothing but the moment.

Take a night-walk through the forest, over hills or along the coast path, and there are perilous things to meet once the torch batteries die and you are alone with the moon's illuminations. Here, shadows are alive.

The beginnings of your story: Once upon a time, in the middle of the night, a small child walked on dark and shadowed pathways, as the sea roared below; as the trees moaned above; as predators rustled and stalked; as perilous faeries wove cruel trickeries.

Let yourself be caught in the spell.

If you live to tell the tale, you will for evermore look at the daytime world with sceptical eyes, and long to walk these nocturnal pathways.

You are a wild thing now, and a story yourself in the telling.

× writing ×

My advice to myself: sit down with a blank page.

Write whatever comes.

Write about the swallows swooping and clicking around the barn. Write about the first joyful Spring we spent here.

Write of the meadow we planted, and the first bold, pink flowers that shot up shouting 'hey!' in the midst of the tentative green-fuzz growth.

Write about the peaceful desert and a beach of souls.

Write of the way spaces change as you walk into them. Write about how you came home. Write about how you grew and how you will be a child again.

Write of ageing and the pain of forgetfulness. Write about babies, smiles, birthdays and undivided attention. Write of presence and being; of silence and deep journeys.

Write of a world that can be saved with a story.

Write of I and us and connectedness…

× the miracle ×

The miracle is not your life.

Trillions of tiny sparks have existed. You are just one of these. Some alighted on tindered ground, burning with a rush – bush fires of life hurrying to destruction. Other sparks fell where the ground was damp – sputtering in the darkness. Short lived. Cruel fate.

Untold souls have lived out their lifespan with the evolutionary integrity of their species. They live and die. They are nothing special.

All these sparks fly, swim, run and crawl in and above the earth and deep below. These are not miracles, any more than you and I. They are the outcome of nature's patient way – thirteen billion years in the making. A trillion sparks from the fire.

The miracle, then, is not your life, but the way you are connected, embedded, attached, intended and united. The miracle is in your personal ecology, the words of your story, and the way you come to the attention of others – if only for a moment.

This one moment is miraculous. All these moments are miraculous.

Sit with this thought. The miracle is not your life. The miracle is love.

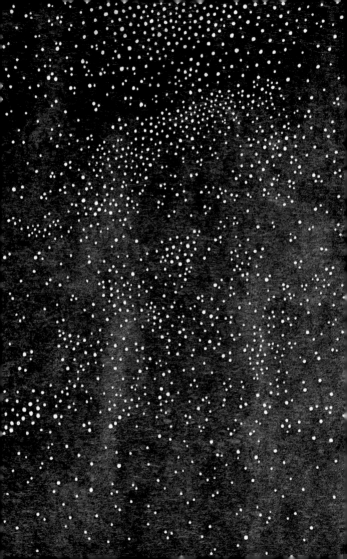

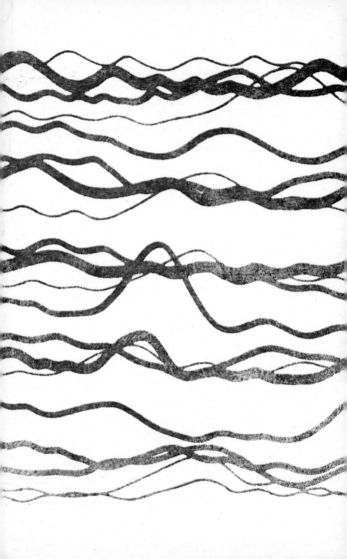

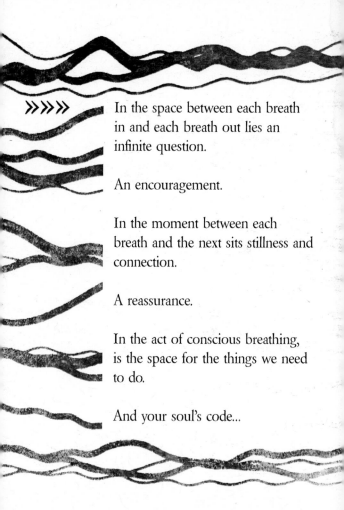

In the space between each breath in and each breath out lies an infinite question.

An encouragement.

In the moment between each breath and the next sits stillness and connection.

A reassurance.

In the act of conscious breathing, is the space for the things we need to do.

And your soul's code...

AFTERWORD

"This is not a time to live without a practice"

Alice Walker

At a basic level, this little book is an encouragement to sustain a beautiful and joyful life, whilst building and sustaining the resilience needed to make some kind of difference in a troubled world. Though these short pieces are my personal responses to these themes, they are intended to inspire and invite you to work with your own soul meditations and secular prayers, and to be mindful of the myriad pieces of joy that this intriguing world offers us.

Just that, really – but there is more to this project, if you'd like to read on...

There is a real need, in our troubled times, for individuals and communities to bring new ways of being, seeing and 'doing' to the world. Being an activist – someone who 'acts' on the world with a clear awareness of **what** needs doing – requires us to be aware of what sustains us as individuals and in our communities; and to know what takes us to our difficult, habitual 'shadow' places.

Alice Walker wrote, "we will be doubly bereft without some form of practice that connects us, in a caring way, to what begins to feel like a dissolving world".

At its best, meditation is a tool to help us to build such a practice. To *see* and *be* in the world in ways that enable us to *do* something important with our lives. Mindfulness – one kind of meditation – helps us to be in the moment, connect with the world and not to spin off into fantasy.

Meditation and contemplation can also help us to recover our 'ground': healing us and bringing us down to earth when the frenzied world spins too fast. Alongside this, body-work like yoga and tai chi – built on ancient wisdoms – can give us the strength to be, as Margaret Wheatley puts it: "Warriors of the Human Spirit".

However, meditation – in our strange, discomforting, late-capitalist civilisation – has become a commodity: something of a trendy shortcut to spiritual awakening. Such practices can take us into the realms of escapism and distraction. It is tempting to hold onto the belief that, if only we can find ways of reaching individual transcendence and enlightenment, then all will be well.

This is *not* the kind of practice that this book is about.

When I think about the earth and my place upon it, I can become despairing and disillusioned. Climate change, in particular, threatens our very way of life; yet we humans have seemed unable to do anything meaningful to respond to this urgent reality. We live in very particular times, in which the problems we face require very different approaches and responses to those of the past.

On the day I wrote this introduction, scientists announced that we have now moved officially into a new geological era – the Anthropocene – the age of human impact. What does this mean? Well, one thing it means is that we can't turn back the clock and return to the wilderness. However, it also requires us to understand what such a shift means for our planet, our fellow lifeforms and for us as human individuals and communities.

So how do we respond?

My first answer is simple: With open eyes, deep realism, courage and encouragement.

In my book, *Soul Manifestos and Pieces of Joy*, I started to outline some ideas that may help us step back from the brink. These were drawn from the fields of ecology and psychology – and many others too.

My sense is that if we are to do this thing, we have to broaden our outlook and reconnect with parts of ourselves we have lost touch with. We can think of these as two forgotten 'realms' of our selfhood. These are our **ecological self**: deeply embedded in the earth we evolved to live upon – and **original soul**: that which carries our individual direction, calling and individuality, whilst connecting us with all other human beings and to the wider world.

In a new book (to be published in 2017) I hope to expand on these ideas in more detail, setting out the beginnings of a practical path forward: a kind of manifesto for ecological, secular soul-making in the 21st Century.

In short, however, I believe that we now have to leave behind the era of 'self-help' and 'personal development' we have lived with for the past half a century or so. We will need to embrace a more uncertain and humble mindset, the tasks of which might be described as 'earth-help', 'community-development' and 'personal embedding'.

These are clumsy phrases, because we haven't yet developed an adequate language of soul-making! As these and other ideas and practices are explored and developed, however, we must trust that more elegant descriptions will follow.

We will need new tools to try out and adapt.

Some of this work has been underway for some time in places like Findhorn and Schumacher College; new social movements like Occupy and Black Lives Matter; in the Transition Towns programmes and developmental work like Margaret Wheatley's Warriors of the Human Spirit and Joanne Macy's Work That Reconnects.

As these and other initiatives are further refined and integrated, there will be less focus on individual development, transcendence and 'happiness'; and more on collective resilience, connectedness and personal grounding. Human sustainability will be the foundation for building new human cultures that are in tune with the planet.

These small soul meditations are mindful prose-poems standing as tools in the space between earth and spirit, hope and despair, individual practice and collective activism. They were written over four years as exploratory waymarks on my own journey through this landscape. They are soulful, I hope, without, needing to rest upon a belief system or religious practice – but they might be considered spiritual, and I am comfortable with that.

One of the ways humans will have to change is for us to shed certainties; to accept forms of language that emerge from disciplines and positions other than the ones we know best. So whilst I might describe these pieces as mindful prose-poems or secular prayers, you might regard them differently! I hope you have enjoyed reading them, and that they might bring you a little nearer to the sensibilities and practices we will all need to touch our wider humanity and magical ecology of the nonhuman world.

Steve Thorp: November 2016

References:

P16: Mary Oliver, Wild Geese, in Dream Work, Atlantic Monthly Press, 1986.
P31: Jon Kabat-Zinn, Full Catastrophe Living, Revised Edition: How to cope with stress, pain and illness using mindfulness meditation, Piatkus, 2013.
P63: Ben Okri, Mental Fight, W&N, 1999.
P75: Alice Walker, We Are the Ones We Have Been Waiting For, W & N, 2007.
P76: Margaret Wheatley, A Path for Warriors for the Human Spirit at
http://margaretwheatley.com/
P77: Steve Thorp: Soul Manifestos and Pieces of Joy, Raw Mixture, 2014.

Steve Thorp www.21soul.co.uk

Steve Thorp is a writer, poet, activist and counsellor working with themes of ecology, creativity and soul-making. He edits Unpsychology Magazine and is the author of Soul Manifestos and Pieces of Joy. In the past he has worked as a teacher and psychotherapist.

Ruth Thorp www.ruththorpstudio.co.uk

Ruth Thorp is an illustrator, designer and children's writer based in Bath. She has published three picture books and had her illustrations published in a number of magazines and journals. Following a BSc in Architecture she worked for ten years as an architectural designer and is now working freelance on a variety of collaborative projects.

Discover more books from Raw Mixture Publishing by visiting
www.rawmixture.co.uk

Raw Mixture Publishing